A Postcard from the Old World

Józef Baran

A Postcard from the Old World

Kraków 2016

Copyright: Józef Baran

Translation: Ewa Hryniewicz-Yarbrough

Editor: Alicja Kuberska

Katarzyna Lisowska

Cover Designer : Agnieszka Herman

Photo: Wojciech Jantos

ISBN 978-1-329-85663-9

2016

Monument

I'll tell the truth
I never loved the dirty
blind village
where I was born in Dedalus's cottage

I watched him angrily
when black and grimy
he stubbornly dug labyrinths
wanting to dig all the way
to the sky

he was a blind mole
staring at the ground
he never raised his head
toward the sun

but my brother and I
often climbed the steps
of the church tower
to glimpse
the roofs of the city
glistening in the distance

we dreamed of flying
so father spent long days
devising wings for us
he owed all the neighbors
and even more deeply thrust
his snout into the ground

today upon returning to the village
with scorched wings
I sometimes stop when I see a mole's mound

this monument erected
to honor my father

A Postcard from the Old World

here's a little farmhouse
propped up
by a withered thistle
with one window staring blindly
at the past

a pile of stones under the window
(or maybe they are only
the stony tears of the old woman
who for years
looked out the window
onto the road
until in the end
she was brought out
to the cemetery
where she became overgrown)

from the bushes of forsaken lilac
droop
the black paws of death

* * *

I am foremost a poet
of shy people
those with the aspen leaf of a smile
stuck to their lips and quaking
at every stronger
flurry of words

those poor relatives of the Danish
prince Hamlet
who have poor diction
and even if with each step they say
to be or not to be
they do it so quietly and hesitantly
that no Shakespeare
has made a tragedy of it

ho ho but who can tell
what lies dormant in those small ones
and never opens its mouth
to the world

what enchanted sleeping knights
wait inside them for the sound of the trumpet
to advance with the flutter of eagle wings
and free the gates of lips
occupied since birth
by enemy guards

The Black Cat

I asked an old man
how his life had passed

he opened
the door wide
after a moment
he shut it

that's how it passed
he answered
(a black cat
jumped into the room
and perched on his shoulder)

A Fable about Cats

walls don't have ears
cats do

God's four-legged
agents
sent to the earth
to spy on Adam

fawningly rubbing
their backs
they slip into the good graces
of our houses

they say nothing
they eavesdrop
the most secret whispers
won't escape the cats' attention
they're everywhere on laps
behind ears underfoot
when we throw them out
they eavesdrop
behind the doorway

at night cats crawl under beds
they light the red lanterns of their eyes
and in their glow
write everything down scrupulously
(in the morning they hide the notebooks in mouse holes)

then at the Last Judgment we're surprised
that God knows everything about us

My Mother's Church

the church was my mother's
theater
there on the stage
before the main altar
actors in chasubles played
their classical parts
so many bells trinkets candelabra were there

the church choir was my mother's
philharmonic
the parish priest conducted it from the altar
the altar boys jingled
the sexton tolled the bells
before the concert

she knelt down
put on her glasses
her fingers rough and thick
cracked from manure
grew slim and beautiful
(for a moment they even
forgot pots and pans)

*

because she liked poetry
she opened her prayer book
and letter by letter
flew toward paradise

Winter

a relentless procession of snowflakes
across desert spaces
between sky and earth

as if the armies of winter
walked and walked and walked
wanting to free us
from the tyranny of grayness

as if heaven sent earth
white telegrams
wanting to reveal the Mystery

but we only hear
the many-tongued whisper of childhood
when life was a strange letter
sent in an envelope
sealed with holiday snow

The First Snow

the first snow is falling
and the quiet music of childhood
rises to the sky
I think of first things
that can't be repeated
of incidents
pure as spring water
that are already behind me
I try to remember
their lushness taste and smell
the first snow is falling
I stand in the window
I feel old

When Behind the Window Snowy Stars Flicker

an old woman reads old letters
and sees her life in a new light
promises which never became flesh
are resurrected from the letters
and flutter like butterflies

the imperfect past
becomes perfect
the girl buried alivc
the one she betrayed
knocks at her heart again
letting her know
she's forgotten nothing
(even though she's covered
with yesterday's snow)

an old woman
dreams of the past
with old letters
she plays solitaire

Air

- for Sophia

you are
like air
invisible yet indispensable
the house breathes you
your countless
poppy-seed chores

you are like silence
which contains everything
and like health

I've never lost you
so
I don't know
what you're really like

An Inventor in Love

one invented the wheel
another built a hydrofoil
the third one took
the first steps on Mars
but I discovered you
on this strange planet
the Earth
and since then each dawn
I'm awakened by
a thought happy
like a lark
that you really exist

The House with Open Walls

through the nerve netted walls
I hear an earthquake in Turkey
a birthday long live long live
the vanilla scent of the most sincere talks of childhood
another attempt at creating a human
the pattering of children above the ceiling Armstrong's
trumpet
the swish of an elevator soaring into the cosmos
the neighbors' quarrel

and also
planes full of images
that won't let me sleep
taking off
from the many airports of memory

I'd like to rest in quiet
but these walls are like shutters
forever ajar
alert like a sleeping hare
with open ears
and eyes

Ballad on All Souls' Day

I often meet my own dead
on the streets at the railway stations of foreign cities
in Dresden Arthur's face flitted by
in an Edinburgh park uncle sat on a bench with a newspaper
I was about to tap him happily on the shoulder
when he turned his changed Scottish face to me
on a subway in Stockholm Mariusz who
had been killed in childhood by a shell found in the rubble
sat down across from me
he pretended not to recognize me
I stared at him
and he jumped off at the next stop

I often meet my dear dead
in a crowd of strange passers by
behind the windows of rushing streetcars
but when they see me they pretend to be someone else
they disguise their familiar walk smile warm gestures
and at once assume indifferent looks
caught red-handed
attempting
a second life.

Trying to Pray at the End of the Century

a dark thought at dawn
that we're only energy's form
for a moment a human in a moment a cloud
a forget-me-not a dog a stone a mound
the meaty mass of matter in the butcher's paws
of chance that probes transforms molds

here February slogs across the barren land
hostile viruses the body inert
and a conviction we're only the body's works
which eats and eliminates eats and eliminates
nowhere any help the faint gleam of faith
in salvation through poetic spells

God of the end of the century ousted
by electronic brains
so uncertain hazy remote help us
through the internet galaxies
give us the tip of your divine finger
as you gave it to Adam in the Sistine
Chapel
a sign that you are still in charge
of all this

Adam and I Have Our Picture Taken Against the Leaning Tower in Pisa

our humanity Adam
is also built on an error
like the leaning tower in Pisa

with the infallibility of death
the colossal
pyramid of fear
(of crashing into the precipice)
boldly rises higher and higher
its peak
reaching the sky

the terrified construction
of water and fire
sawed through
at the base

Posing for a Photograph

we want to immortalize ourselves against the ruins
but we are only negatives
which in a moment will dissolve
undeveloped
like those who posed here
before us
and those after us

only the temple of Apollo
which has stood here for four thousand years
will come out clear

On the Death of Uncle Bach a Taxidermist

when he came for Uncle at daybreak
to take the Final Measure of his soul
the whole household was asleep
only the mare neighed in the stable

(oh yes death is a perfect criminal
or maybe a wardrobe assistant
who replaces the body's worn out earthly outfits
since up there new ones have been prepared)

Uncle loved to stuff hawks
now he is a dummy stuffed by death
the house is full of relatives prattling off the rosary
the birds stare blankly with their glass eyes

grandchildren whisper something in Grandpa broke down
the old ones can't add anything else to death
behind the window dusk has lost itself in conjecture
Aunt spreads her arms helplessly

she tells again and again how he was alive yesterday
she stands frozen at the abyss in which nothing can be seen
where at dawn all traces of Uncle went missing
the body under the cover only an earthly forgery

like others I too lift the sheet
as if I wanted to unveil the mystery
but since the beginning of the world
no one who's lived here has accomplished that

Borzęcin 1991

Entropy

from a sailing boat
I watched fire
it raged it bristled it sparked
the red turkey cock
of its flames
threatening to upset
the Majesty of the Sea

it ran along the shore
of a small island
in Skorgarden
and like a fury
it leapt away
from the silent indifference of the water
which no matter what
would swallow its verbosity

looking at the fire
I felt sorry
for myself

* * *

I write
increasingly light
poems
casting off
the ballast of reality
as if from a balloon

to let them soar
higher and higher
the pure
transparent lyrics
filled only with eternity

Woman with Cancer

She joins us at the table
And she burns from head to toe
But we sit next to her as if nothing had happened
With mouths full of unnecessary words

Someone pulls back a tiny bit
To stay clear of the fire
Someone else puts on an ice shell
Pretending not to know

She talks and talks and talks
As if she wanted to talk down her ill fortune
And we don't know if we should laugh with her
Or cry over her

We don't know how to help her
When she is all in a fiery hoop
Trying in vain to escape
To another person

The earth burns under her feet
The sky burns over her head
The words burn in her mouth
Her whole world is on fire

She'd like to jump out of her burning body
But she doesn't know how

And the Waters Keep Flowing

I returned from my journey
a gray Don Quixote
without fortune or fame
with a bag full of phantoms
the wealth of a squire of errant words
who raced shadows and fought windmills
whose youth slipped by like a day
and whose world seeped through his fingers

but maybe I have never left here
where all roads have their beginnings

and everything I encountered
was only a delusion
a phantasmagoria from my childhood books

I muse by the river
there's calm after the storms and howls
and one mask after another
falls from my face
into the waters of the Uszwica that keep flowing and
flowing

A Father's Psalm

my daughter and I are still picking mushrooms
together in the Czarnawa woods
hooting and calling from a distance
but her own woods
bristling with thorns
tempting with berries
draw her in more and more deeply

one day she'll flit past
vanish behind pines
and only the beguiling trees
will rustle rustle rustle

"where are you, Daddy?"
she'll cry
to hear only the echo of her own voice

An X-Ray

When on my bike
I pass in the summer sun
the family cemetery
the eyes
of all my own dead
pierce me through
projecting
in the flash of a second
the whole nothingness
of My Royal Highness
the Body

Learning From an Ant

when I again lose sight of purpose
since it seems
that all our earthly efforts
are good for nothing

I watch with admiration
an anonymous ant:
the fortune's miniature
bodybuilder
lugging uphill
a seed of Faith

with such determination
as if on it depended
whether the earth will continue
to turn

In Praise of Life

we were returning from a funeral

before us
as far as our eyes could see
life spread
and blossomed
with a million
possibilities
the most ordinary under the sun
which had faded
under the dead person's eyelids

now newly discovered
they sparkled
with the colors of the rainbow

how incomprehensible
is death's wastefulness

Mother

To J. L., whose son died of AIDS

she held his hand in her warm palm
leading him across the narrowing footbridge
of his body
to the other side
of the pole

when she moistened his lips
she whispered into his ear:
“just a little longer
the great peace is coming
it’ll free you from suffering”

he was a weak child again
led to the end of the polar night
beyond which only nothingness waited
with an angel’s icy hand

to this day she’s never returned
she still slogs through snowdrifts
lonely more lonely than her son
who left holding on
to her hand

Over Tadeusz Makowski's Paintings*

we stop here sometimes
in the cozy shrines of solitude
we yearn for little streets
with the most real moon
suspended over the tower
for the creaking gates opened
with the morning sigh of the town hall clock
where graying mothers
guard our long faded smiles

we remember paradise
those winged angels
first girlfriends
we pine for the old attic
where once we found
a rusty Austrian bayonet

a bunch of keys
to a hundred unknown gates
jingles in our pockets
the world is still
a tale from the Arabian Nights

and everything
literally everything
may happen

*Tadeusz Makowski, a Polish painter (1882-1932), known for lyricism and naïve realism in his portrayal of children.

A Trip

I forgot everything
after I had settled in
an old-fashioned stage coach of the novel
driven by Henry James

before me still 500 pages
of wandering through the world
which assumes
it'll remain forever the same
and that's why so leisurely
it reveals
detail after detail

just now I am
near London
in the 19th century
in an old country house
where summer light begins its slow departure
shadows grow long on thick grass
and few hours in life
are more pleasant
than the time of the ritual
known as afternoon tea

How far from there
to the 21st century
to Krakow
and to me on a hospital bed
waiting for surgery

once upon a time
in the novel's faraway land

The Hat

at the beginning there was a hat
a circus hat
from which
to his own amazement
God pulled out himself

then he kept sticking his hand
in the hat
and for six days in a row
pulled out Heaven and Earth
as well as the five proofs
of his own existence

planets like ping-pong balls
leaped out of
the magic hat
and God
with his divine fingers
made each one spin

the planets multiplied
with terrifying speed
while he
hustled as if in boiling water
in the middle of the spinning planetarium
careful not to let even one drop off his finger

meanwhile in the audience
Adam and Eve had already been sitting
and to tell the truth
they couldn't believe
their own eyes

Commandments

like a cat you will walk
your own paths
barefooted
cutting your feet on sharp stones
to feel even more painfully
the separateness of your life

ready-made bibles
won't be sufficient for you
nor other people's holy writs

at roadside stops
in the sweat of your imagination
you'll be writing down
the private Gospel of Life

for your defense
you'll only have
the madman's papers
of poetry

Cosmic Diptych

1. At the Shore

at the shore
of the roaring Cosmos
in the flares of suns and stars
we children of the Earth bustle
making sandcastles
fortresses houses
borders of countries

waves rush swishing
they shatter our beliefs
they sweep our joys
sorrows civilizations
city towers
with the comets' tail

at the shore
of the roaring ocean
called Cosmos
our lives
the slight sparks
sending the SOS
into darkness

2. A Spark

isn't it a miracle
this spark of warm life
the roe laid by God
at the bottom of
the empty expanse

where we kneel
against the background of cold galaxies
and indifferent Cosmos
blowing on it and sustaining it
to keep off the chill wind from the stars

isn't it a miracle
to endure like that
believing till the last breath
in its divine power

Errata

with years
the errata
expands
outgrowing the work

time
catches errors
with the ruthlessness
of a cosmic
proofreader

Girl with Wings

a girl with a violoncello on her back
one among hundreds of passers-by
attached to the earth
by gravity
plods across Planty Park

suddenly
she turns into the entrance
of a glass building
painted with music

where gracefully
before an amazed audience
she breaks off from the earth
and flies high far away
beyond Mozart's seven clouds

City on a Hot Day

faded in the heat
the spectral apparitions
of stone phantoms
posters cars crowds
imitating
life

the overexposed film
the undisguised
imitation of a shadow play

the deserted stage of the market square
though the disappointed gawkers
still wait for
the Grand Spectacle

but it's taking place now
where summer
recites its lush monologues
of grasses flowers birds
in the mountains
forests gardens

where the World's Great Stage
has been moved

and where things most important
under the sun are acted out
with the Earth and the Sun
in leading roles

Forest Echology

in the Czarnow forest
eternity
frolics with nothingness
in the shape of a transparent dragonfly

the beginning plays
hide-and-seek
with the end
calling
from behind the tree trunks

the effect
asks about the cause
but
it hears only
the echo
of its own voice

while the waters of life
keep flowing
the dark swellings
under the roots of oaks and pines

Still Here?

"Still here?"
sighs Mother awakened
at dawn by the bells
she's locked in the body's cell
open only to memories
glowing from far away
through the peephole of memory
each time with different brightness

she listens
for the mysterious sound
of the belfry
flowing
from the other world
where she will be welcomed
by Boluś and Staś
my two brothers who died prematurely
they will take her by her hands
and lead her
across darkness
over the footbridge of light

The Doctor Says It's the Beginning of Hypertension

they don't let me sleep
they get me up
to hammer out the scythe
to mow meadows
though in Krakow
you will find no meadows
only concrete and smog

my peasant ancestors
the early birds
grandmas and grandpas
who bustle
in my genes
walk around in my head
don't let me sleep
on spring mornings

earlier and earlier
they wake me up
calling me to return
under our apple tree
from which I fell off
far and long ago
the apple displayed
in the stalls of the city

Metamorphoses

it seemed
that any moment now
death will catch up
with life
when a dead stone turned
into a swallow
and escaped
the shell of winter broke
and larks flew out of it
raising the toast
to the glory of the Creator
and all creation
a dead pit
swiftly shot
shoots
great –grandmother
changed into
her granddaughter
and the crucified Christ
from the roadside shrine
rose
above the woods
in the woods
eternal light
like echo
resounds
with snowdrops
and the waters of life
keep flowing
in the swollen veins
under the tree roots

Self-portrait with a Prickly Pear (a fifty-year old poet looks at himself in a hotel mirror)

I survived
though so many stronger than I
were killed by this terrible
sensitivity I succumbed to so often

over the years I grew thick skin
and chitin claws
I endured poverty in Borzecin
Asian flu a few neuroses

I often licked myself back to shape
by a hair's breadth I dodged cancer
a street accident
a heart attack
I didn't drink myself
to death

I survived
and brought myself
to a hotel mirror
in this poorly resistant
photosensitive vessel
which at dawn
fills itself with cosmos
in this fragile shell
glued with contradictions
exposed to cracks shocks
endless spills

I survived
I *homo sapiens poeticus*
an extinct species
in this electronic epoch
I have automatic wings
that if necessary
can be instantly shut
in the box that has
the epoch's camouflage

over the years I've learned
to defend myself successfully
against myself
to guard access to myself
like a thorny
prickly pear

I survived
it's almost a miracle

after half a century
I stand in the hotel mirror
alive and whole
surprised at myself

so many times it seemed
that I wouldn't carry even a single day
in this fragile shell of the soul
subject to the whims of the ocean

Portrait of a Woman Combing Her Hair

with hair down
she runs through the corridor
toward the back
of the express train: the birth-death line
as if she wanted to stop
the escaping gardens
the ribbon of childhood
the wedding veil
as if she wanted to turn back time
which has kidnapped her
her rapid breathing
scuffles with
the rattling wheels

she runs against the current of her reflection
but it carries away
her legs her hair
and her futile race
which slows down
from year to year

a fifty-year old woman
standing before a mirror

A Late Response to Emily Dickinson's Letters

welcome dear Emily
in my garden in Borzecin
where after a hundred and fifty years
your letters from the world have reached me
the lights of a long vanished planet

over my head a woodpecker
hammers his home in a pear tree
and the blue of the sky is so immaculate
that it's a reproach to creation

I'm happy that we think alike
really Great Events
aren't the noisy
boasts of an epoch
but a sparrow's delight
in a bread crumb
the arrival of spring
so marvelous and unexpected
that you don't know what to do with your heart

I sinned complaining that fate
brought me too few changes
since even what I have
is too much of too much
too many conversations faces

I overlooked so many treasures
the kaleidoscopes of travels twinkled
while you watched
violets breaking through grass
and in each moment you caught
Eternity's reflection

welcome dear Emily
you put me to shame
you beautiful sprite
cricket in the garden
your singing selflessly accompanies
the daily earthly bustling

Ballad about Immigrants

they wake up in the middle of the night
cut off from the homeland's umbilical cord
with gagged mouths
not feeling the ground
under their feet

for a while longer
the sunken Titanic of childhood
looms before them

the language has already been transplanted
the brain is being transplanted
only the heart transplant
has not been successful
and though it's old and too big
they'll have to die with it

scales drop off their eyes
and they understand
that the true destiny
is never ending exile
from the familiar places
beginning with the magic
horizon of childhood
accepting the thought
that death is also immigration
beyond the last border of the body

When I Opened a Box of Black Shoe Polish

the smell
of the shoe polish
resurrects my father
in his tall boots
gray smoke emerges
which once more
conjures up a home
on Sunday

in the doorway
my brother and I busily
shine our church shoes
as the bells toll
for high mass

Mother
in high heels
still so young

the cat rubs against my feet
and the world looks
as if it just
had been painted
with the May sun

all that closed in a box
for a moment smelled like heaven

To My Granddaughter

little ray
ray of hope
like a spear of light

little cosmonaut
in the rocket of your baby carriage
ready for takeoff
to the distant planet of the future

little Buddha with a mysterious smile
with at least one particle of life
I'll catch you
fly away
escape death

A Fable about Grandmothers

they are born the third time
in the halo of silver hair
from their grandchildren
and learn to take first steps
then they go with them
to first communion

it's almost impossible to imagine
that they weren't grandmothers before
eternal in their serenity
who shone shine and will shine
even if everything has changed for good

their husbands are long gone
or fed up with life
with disgust they drink
the beer they have brewed

while they re-incarnated at the source
untiring housekeepers of life
divide it justly and evenly
among their grandchildren

they look as if they were to live eternally
they simply don't notice death
though it peers into their eyes
after all they have so much to do
in their new incarnation

* * *

awake at three in the morning
I listen to the starry barking of
February dogs
and think how strange
and unlike each other
my lives have been

it's as if I had been reborn
in successive incarnations
and died without an echo
all of that lasted
whole centuries
and was like the crack of a whip

on various planets
I took on the hues
of such different tunes of being
that I can't help but wonder
what I have in common
with that boy
from the Paleolithic era
who was roped to the cow's tail

thousands of faces
millions of incidents
sunken in me
as if in the titanic
loom at the bottom of the ocean
and sometimes phosphoresce in memory

be merry sorrow be merry
weep joy weep
everything so propitiously
converged into a whole
about which I understand
next to nothing

November Ballad

November is an unloved woman
who complains and complains
she lets her hair down before a mirror
and no longer waits

she’s read all the letters from trees
and in none found something for herself
they lie scattered at her feet
and the wind blows them up and down

she’s looked at the stars full of sorrow
intended for the rest of her life
she laughs the madwoman’s laughter
so no one knows what she hides

A Poet's Prayer

after many years I see
that time is
an evil sorcerer
who changes beautiful girls
into old women with walking sticks
stars into grains of sand
and butterflies into hideous monsters

it curses with transience
everything it encounters
on its way

grant me God for the longest time
the power of a good wizard
let me at least for a moment
break the spell
from the world
restore enchantment
to life
and change a toad
into a beautiful princess again

Only So Much

1

a vain
effort
to imagine
life after life

the result known in advance

as if a feather
tried to pierce
the tunnel
of a gale

a hopeless effort
to imagine
yourself
without the world

although the world
managed without me
for billions of years

and will continue to do so

2

billions of dew drops
glittering in the sun

bells of millet
jingling in a procession
near the forest

the merry-go-round of leaves
whirling in your head
when you stand
under the Tree of the Universe

the twinkling of stars
as if Infinity
watched us
with innumerable eyes

the improbable
recurrence of
birth
and death

until
the head
spins

The Last Leap

dying is only falling
from the body's Mont Blanc

a leap for it all
into voracious nothingness

believing that after
we cross the barrier of life
the parachute of the soul
will open on its own

STEVE YARBROUGH*

A Poet of Shy People

I began reading Jozef Baran's poems the way poems should be read – gradually, slowly, savoring each one as my wife Ewa finished translating it. I was immediately struck by their straightforward beauty, by their ability to move and speak to the heart, and by their unfashionable accessibility. About a year after Ewa began working on these translations, Jozef came to visit us in Fresno, California, and to do a reading at the university where I teach. During the week that he stayed with us I discovered that I liked the poet as much as the poetry. An unpretentious man with a self-deprecating sense of humor, he won me over instantly, just as his work won over the large audience that gathered for his reading.

I found out that Jozef and I had a lot in common. I was born in the Mississippi Delta, where my father and grandfather toiled in the cotton fields. Baran was born in a village in southern Poland, the fact responsible for some critics' attempts to place him in the peasant poetry tradition. Such reductionist categories that assign poets and writers into the ghettoes of region, class or gender appeal to academics and critics because they give them the impression that the unruly beast of literature can be reined in and tamed. But like many other writers, Baran resists attempts at neat categorization. If there's anything of peasant provenance in his poetry, it's his tenderness toward the earth and the natural world and his stubborn, even defiant independence from literary fads and trends. Whatever label we use to describe Baran's poetry, we instantly have to come up with its opposite. There's amazement at the beauty of the world and anguish over its horrors; there's ecstasy and pain, elation and melancholy, faith and doubt.

If Baran has a poetic creed, it can be found in these lines:

I am foremost a poet
of shy people
those with the aspen leaf of a smile

While he often writes of those who either can't, or won't, speak on their own behalf, he is never shy himself – if by shy, we mean someone who is afraid to meet experience head-on, to risk an extended encounter with the other.

The willingness to embrace risk, to step beyond the borders, for instance, of class and gender, to write from a perspective other than his own – these are among Baran's defining traits as a poet. One of his most moving poems, to my way of thinking, is about a woman being consumed by cancer. Rather than hide, as so many others might, behind the veil of irony, Baran confronts emotion here with shocking directness:

And she burns from head to toe
But we sit next to her as if nothing had happened
With mouths full of unnecessary words

Someone pulls back a tiny bit
To stay clear of the fire
Someone else puts on an ice shell
Pretending not to know

She talks and talks and talks
As if she wanted to talk down her ill fortune
And we don't know if we should laugh with her
Or cry over her

As this poem so powerfully illustrates, Baran's poetry is a poetry of empathy. Each encounter – even the moment's observation of an ant "lugging uphill/a seed of faith" – is rife with possibility, if we can only move beyond our own narrow confines. This, in the end, is the task this poet of shy people has set for himself, and it is one at which he succeeds beautifully.

* **Steve Yarbrough**. *American novelist, and essayist, professor at Emerson College in Boston.*

Contents

www.ingramcontent.com/pod-product-compliance
Ingram Content Group UK Ltd.
Pitfield, Milton Keynes, MK11 3LW, UK
UKHW041915190726
13854UKWH00003B/1257

9 781329 856639